SIDE A
alemany bay window ▶
◀ redwood coast record crate
SIDE B

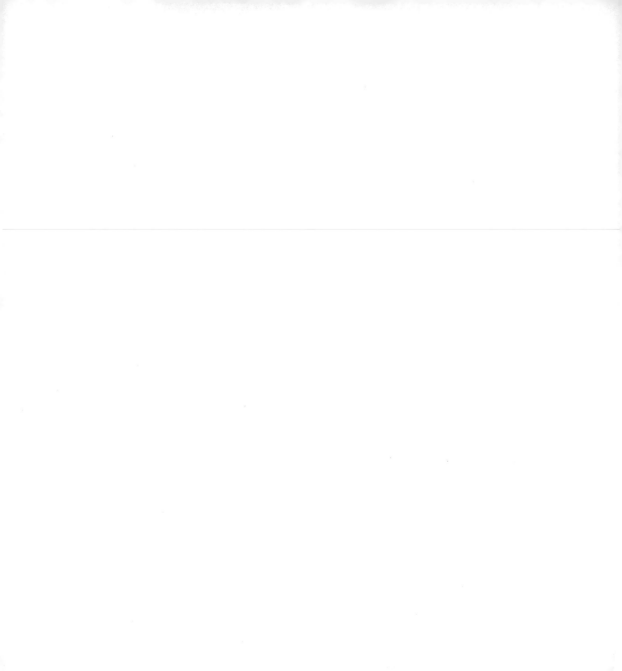

alemany bay window

David Maduli

Sampaguita
Press

for

Blezilda S. Maduli
/1945-2008/

and

Edralin J. Maduli
/1944-2022/

I think it was in June...you were born August. Your mom was here. That was a long time. We grab this house because your mom was pregnant with you.

The people in here are all kinds of nationalities, they have Swedish, they have Italian, they have Irish, and just few Filipino families. There was about three of them. I thought this place before was like they don't want anyone moving in here, I thought it was just very high class neighborhood.

When we move in here, this family in here on the corner, they are Irish...and every time we go out they are watching us. How we move around, how we dress up ourselves, you know because we walk around. They were just curious you know because not many Filipinos live in here, that's why.

But then when we got to know them they were all welcome, they were all nice after a while.

They are all gone now.

—Lola Encarnación Soriano

Contents

8   St. Mary's Park   [Tempo rubato.]
9   Ancestory
10 Directions, *by car from the East Bay*
12 thru triple stage darkness
13 innerlude: *insomnia*
14 Directions, *continued*
      / The Park Bell
22 Visiting Hours Over
25 innerlude: *bay bridge {inverted}*
26 Frisco Silent Film Reel
27 SF Urban Legend
29 Ode to the Ollie, Landing on a Line by Teju Cole
30 Global Positioning System
31 Directions, *reprise*
33 foundation
34 St. Mary's Park   [Repeat and fade.]

St. Mary's Park   [Tempo rubato.]

on a Mission the swift sunstone revolves
                 Dream One engraves each block by hand
                               spraycan sighs unwrap walls

                                  years short moments tall
                 hearts compress curb cracks expand
          on a Mission the swift sunstone revolves

Lolo's ghost cane drags hardwood halls
                 avocado cones drip down homeland
                             spraycan sighs unwrap walls

                       garden breathes Lola waters all
              this house leaks stories hourglass spits sand
on a Mission the swift sunstone revolves

            truth crystallizes youth dissolves
                 living room rug nudge mother's cold hand
                               spraycan sighs unwrap walls

                       wishes big inside boy small
             coroner van takes Mom leaves man
         on a Mission the swift sunstone revolves

spraycan's sigh unwraps walls

Ancestory

I come from Bataan's flamethrower sun
Searing Lolo as he marched bayonet
At his back then packed in a boxcar
Concentration camp concertina terminus

Dirt floor bamboo hut soup kalabaw scraps
Pelagra stew cups of malaria
Officer's insignia Pangasinan infidelity Citizenship chicanery
Thirty-three months in another prison camp

In another war
I come from Lola's shout of surprise
When her husband came home again
I come from Lingayen Gulf blue crabs in a pot

Behind a pandesal bakery I come from a chest high heap
Of snails picked from paddy's seedlings
Bunching onions in a Monterey County field racing tractors
Wrenches and grease

A bay window on a cluster of streets bent
To form a bell beyond the boundary
Of a tourist map of The City. I come from the fog
That has no name. What is a grandchild?

It is saltwater's arabesque. What is ancestry? It is
The grapefruit dawn after earthquake
Aftershocks. What is homeland? This poem buried
In the backyard under Lola's bedroom window.

Directions, *by car from the East Bay*

Wake up in your southside apartment around noon feeling slightly queasy. You're late. Step out over banana slugs, past what's left of the bamboo those old Vietnamese ladies keep cutting and stealing when no one's home, past the storage space homie broke into and stayed all week, past the big front house.

        Move the sleeping housemate's car that's blocking yours in. Open your passenger door in order to unlock the driver's side. Gas tank's on E in the Hyundai Excel. Orange light isn't on yet, should be enough.

Drive city streets to pick up your older sister Denise after her CBEST at Oakland Tech. She was back from the Peace Corps for two months when her old car died. Nod as she opens the door and drops her bag on the seat.

Feel a pain in your temples coming on. Hop on 24, there's already traffic to The City on a Saturday. Crack the windows for air. Ignore concerned looks from your sister. Juggle the gas and clutch through the MacArthur Maze. Let two cars cut you off before leaning on the steering column and hugging the bumper in front of you.

Scrounge up coins from the cup holders, the ashtray. Take the bill your sister hands you. Pay the $2 toll. Juggle first and second gears through the metering lights. On the ramp to the upper deck of the Bay Bridge see darkness creeping in both sides of your vision. Open the windows all the way to let in the summer chill.

Grip the steering wheel as hard as you can. Alternate between deep breaths and fast shallows. Wipe the damp from your temples and throw your beanie in the back seat. The dark clouds stop moving toward your lane but are still collecting, waiting. Your sister's asking, *Are you ok?* but just shake your head and will the car forward before you black out.

thru triple stage darkness

you hear a melody in the key of maritime distress
off the coast of nothingness. or is it sade's absinthe lament.

or charlie hunter speedballin with guitar and bass down a single
eight-string axe. or a church choir of termites amplified

on a thousand speakers in stereo surround. or is it the devil.
you still shade your salvation with aviators and heave a black

duffel full of dopefiend beat and you know what?
you ain't scared well maybe just a praying mantis' wing

and you have dead presidents in your pocket and a silver cross
and debt. sense you're not alone, know you're not in

a crowd. feel a presence in front of you and an absence
behind that breathes just as cancerous if that makes sense—

my god, my god. each fingernail caked with cavern
is a prayer. sanctity is made with theremin and traction.

snow is a summer kiss. now you begin to place the source
and tenor of the instrument as it wraps you smooth and pliable,

pythonic. you hear it from every all: a steelpan. rusted. probably torch-
welded from an oil drum. sponge and rubber-headed sticks

strike each hit as you cry out in harmony. another someday
is the only light you carry.

innerlude: *insomnia*

this past wednesday Lola woke up at one-thirty a.m. and there was a bright circle on the ceiling right above her head and she closed and opened her eyes, called out, walked the railing down the hall to the bathroom and back, waved the beam of her flashlight wildly and the light was still there. and she fell asleep and woke at her usual morning hour and counted all the decades she had lived here in this house and never seen anything like that

Directions, *continued*

Wake up. You're on Treasure Island parked by the Coast Guard gate. The view of The City is astonishingly clear. Denise is outside watching the sun set. Tilt the driver's seat up as she clicks her seat belt, pop the clutch and press the gas back towards the bridge. Recall that time in Unit 1 when the stress was thick as Daly City fog—you drove the crew to the TL to catch Shingo and the Cooltempo DJs at an underground spot. Pankaj was riding shotgun, window cracked to the crisp night; Gene was wondering why you were circling the same downtown blocks endlessly; two floormates who tagged along were rapping loud to *Midnight Marauders*. The muscle memory of that drive will keep you from crashing now—flip on "Oh My God" in the cassette deck and use your knees to steady the wheel.

The Park Bell

The bedrock is ancient. It undulates in earthquakes but does not crack. The hill—steep enough to send a bicycle novice into rose thorns—faces another hill which in a previous incarnation heaved a mental hospital, sprawling pink. The hills bow to each other as the afternoon fog fills the reach between.

Stay on 80 past the curve of the county jail, the Gap billboard, Potrero Hill, Army Street. Bend right onto 280 by the graffiti tribute to Dream at the Alemany Flea Market, exit Alemany Street. Right at the stop sign and you're on Justin. Cut left through the bell on College, it takes too long to go all the way around. Pull in the driveway and set the parking brake. Lola will hear you and press the Genie from upstairs to open the garage door.

Lola's house stands on Justin Drive at the upper curve of the bell, its shoulder.

The kiss of the house, the embrace of the curled front stairs. The bay window's gaze.

It's dark outside now, go upstairs and curl into bed, in the room you and your sister slept summers and holidays, where you two would make so much noise after bedtime Lola would come out in the hallway and *Ssssst!!* only making you laugh harder. The room where Lolo used to watch *The Love Boat* in his red velvet easy chair while you sat at his feet.

Federico David Soriano was a veteran of WWII and Korea and a prisoner of war in both. Those stints would get him and his family to the US in 1955, ten years before the floodgates opened with the Immigration Act, before other family members were petitioned to come. "Wake up," Denise nudged one summer morning in 1989 after returning from the hospital we visited daily. "Grandpa died. You missed breakfast." It had only been a month after we returned from a four-year sojourn overseas. Mom would say later that he waited for us to come back. A 21-gun salute recoiled across the ridge at Skylawn.

In the hallway are many frames from his military service: The Bronze Star Medal *for meritorious achievement in ground operations against the enemy, Philippine Islands, 1942.* The Purple Heart. The Army Commendation Medal. There is a photo of him and Lola, Mom and Uncle Eddie in front of their brick quarters in Ft. Benning, Georgia, his first assignment in the states. Uncle Eddie is wearing a bow tie and a slate blue blazer that matches Lola's dress. Mom's wearing white gloves and smiling, the only one whose teeth are showing. Both grandparents have the same smirks to the right corner of their mouths, but Lolo still manages to look stern with his crew cut and Army dress blues.

Wake up many hours later, already late at night. Your sister is asleep. Lola has arroz caldo waiting, warm on the stove. The advice nurse on the phone tells you it was a stomach virus. Begin to recall the late eats you had coming from the jazz set at Yoshi's on Claremont twenty-four hours ago.

The slight slope, like gravity is off. The trellis built by Uncle Eddie, Dad and me. All those pieces of wood we took turns cutting with a hand saw. The brick planter in the center where there was a lemon tree we climbed as kids. Then cut down and replanted with a calamansi tree. Then removed and paved over. The big deck we played fishing games from. Torn down and replaced with the small deck. The four steps, turn, then three more. The last

step that Lola missed, hit her head on the ground. The stain on the concrete, the flurry of cousin Macoy carrying her to the garage, the ambulance.

The paramedics hauling ass on Mission then diverting away from St. Luke's Hospital down Cesar Chavez to the ER at General. The flowers, the colors. Roses. Camellias. Bees.

The garden that Lola was weeding, watering when Mom died on the living room floor.

Curse the orange creamsicle shake—who mixes citrus with dairy? And the fries covered with cheese and chili that had probably been sitting on the counter all day. Swear off the Smokehouse on Telegraph—even though you know you will be back there soon.

Magnets from Lola's travels fill up the freezer door. At some point my sister and I started buying magnets at souvenir stands or airports in other cities and countries we visited to gift to her collection. On the counter Lola has thawed salmon. The colander is full of rinsed bok choy, tomato, okra. Ginger, garlic and onion rest on the chopping board. Her sinigang, as always, will be sour with lemon.

The year I lived with Lola after college, I acclimated to her no-salt cooking, doctor's firm directive. So much so that it became difficult to eat in restaurants because everything was so salty. She's a centenarian now, the doctor says she can eat whatever she wants. We just need to make sure she eats.

Be easy, you have another whole day and night until your summer
job at Garfield Elementary starts on Monday.

The garage has sheltered every member of this family who immigrated—
    papers or none—over the course of four decades.

Uncle Rudi built a bedroom in the garage. When he moved downtown to Minna Street a nun stayed
    there, then a "beauty operator." Uncle Ben came from the Philippines and added an extension.
    When it was earthquake-proofed decades later an SF city inspector cited: *insufficient ventilation*.
    For five years, a skeleton of a frame.

The garage may or may not have been a graveyard
    for abandoned cars.

A green snake lived in the garage. It stayed hugging the foundation til one day
    it slithered down the driveway and the neighbor lady ran out
    and stomped it in the street with a two by four.

The garage: for three generations the kids never want to go down there alone.

Uncle Rudi will not go in the garage at all.

Sink back into the twin size mattress. You are home.

Living room. Because of this room, I know: Christmas tree. Fireplace. Fireworks on a clear July 4th

over Twin Peaks. Central heating. Bay window. Double paned glass. Crown molding. Vaulted.

French doors. Freeze dance. What Harley-Davidsons sound like. Post-mortem. Body bag. Dead.

What that feels like. A mother who lived to see six great-grandchildren. Who outlived her daughter.

What that sounds like.

This house,

Amalgamation of redwood plaster stucco metal glass
Dry rot asbestos termites
Miscarriages rosaries boiling water
Tomatoes and green beans still wet
In the colander in the sink
By the window through which
You can see Lola watering the camellias
The sun glaring intently above the eucalyptus grove
From which a sharp-shinned hawk watches
Circles and falls.

Visiting Hours Over

—ER, SF General, Tuesday April 23

8:07pm   head nurse scours three rooms
she was here a second ago
find Lola in the hallway
beside five more
occupied gurneys

8:09pm   her hand is warm
eyes full
grip strong: *get me*
a pillow

8:43pm   morphine
red pattern on sheet blooms slow
she smiles
at photos of her great grandchildren
the stretchers, sheriffs and nurses passing
are the late afternoon fog that always reaches
outer mission last

9:30pm   the tall man
parked next to her
has a mesh bag over his head
inside it is potrero hill
light snores
handcuffs jangle in tune

9:58pm   code 900
equals cleared hallway
locked doors
six family members in a small room
she sees the paramedics pass
through oxygen

10:16pm   the woman they usher to the only empty seat
last saw her son under an SUV

11:09pm   staples
for paperwork
back of head
neck
family

11:51pm   fuck this hallway to heaven
why is Lola still lined up here?

12:22am		she gets a 4th floor room
		the woman on the other side of the curtain
		cusses out the nurse
		pees on the floor

12:53am		doctor is optimistic
		but her face at the word surgery
		painted with end

1:37am		fourth cat scan since ambulance
		"findings" in her brain
		are stable
		Lola is yelling at us for staying
		hates when we drive at night

2:13am		bataan standard time
		this winter's firing squad only grazes
		third thoracic vertebra separated into archipelago
		Lola will carry to her centennial
		bones older than this city block

innerlude: *bay bridge {inverted}*

{across time
swifting thru mazes of eight story
tenements invisible under nightly blackouts
feel their stare, their mass
their groan

at some corners my people have lit
streetfires with garbage
sneering limbs of ember strobe
frowns on hidden highrises

heavens
help us find our way
}

Frisco Silent Film Reel

Lolo, you survived a death march, two p.o.w. camps in two different wars, death of a third child before he was three months old, birth of another to a housekeeper in the barracks, Lola back in the province with two kids, boat to guam then cross pacific through the golden gate to drive down south one night leaving miscarried fourth in a motel bin, segregation-era georgia, retired civilian monotony, and a stroke that froze most your right side; but you never talked about these things, in fact you never talked that much at all

what your silence taught me was to get out of hospitals fast as you can, don't say anything to Lola when you lose a $100 bill, the best reception on the tv during fantasy island is when you angle the rabbit ears toward the window, and the avocado ice cream at mitchell's is worth walking six blocks with a cane and the use of only one leg

SF Urban Legend

Your family's weekend drive from Lola's house in Outer Mission
        To the Presidio is a jagged roiling run
                Impossible to trace by the tourists you spy lining

Up to catch a cable car down San Francisco's
        Hilly grid. Past Glen Park station the road
                Hairpins in the shadows of Twin Peaks

Waterfalls into West Portal then sinks into the canyons and
        Gauntlet of trees around McAteer High. The grid
                Is true here, you track the alphabetic order

Of streets Quintara Pacheco Ortega Noriega Moraga
        Lawton Kirkham Judah Irving into Golden Gate Park
                From one side to the other is not a straight line more like

A half-remembered dream dozing in and out between joggers
        And bicyclists and jarring you onto Arguello and another grid up
                Geary Clement where you pull over

For a box of fresh steamed siopao tied with pink
        String then the steepest ridge into the old army
                Base where you take photos with your sister

Perching on cannons and standing barely taller
        Than cannon balls. Then around to the
                Old fort under the famous bridge

Where dad folds down the back of the Volvo
>	Mom opens the box still warm and dotted with moisture
>>	You watch the waves and the seagulls

Feed them the sticky sweet blood-pink
>	Pork, only eating the chewy
>>	White bun. You always drift

Asleep on the ride home head rocking and
>	Bumping slightly on the window as dusk
>>	Overtakes you. Years later you tell college friends

The story of the Golden Gate
>	Park Runners. As you drive through
>>	The trees a figure appears jogging

Next to your window. You speed up and
>	Even faster still and the runner is still
>>	There beside you

As you twist and turn and it is nearly pitch dark
>	Except what's in front of your headlights
>>	You can't shake the runner even if

You mash the gas to the carpet and they don't
>	Stop running and the ghosts keep
>>	Slipping the lakes and windmills and

Buffalo meadows until this San Francisco
>	And every San Francisco is long gone
>>	*Come run grandson, on another fog we will rest.*

Ode to the Ollie, Landing on a Line by Teju Cole

the first scrape and drag of the
skateboard's tail is a striking match
one motion two feet to griptape
four wheels from driveway to

deep space street
enough vibration between rocky asphalt
and polyurethane wheels to circulate

blood from feet to fingertips to cumulus clouds
to pedestrians downhill it sounds like a strafing
curb is a looming island

gather spirits from pine and aluminum
pop of the tail is the sidewalk's
fingers snapping

lunge at the cracks in air
above the brick waves
disappearing into the wrought iron gate

the day offers no shade or shadows
each morning is the beginning of a summer
heavy waters above and flowing waters below

Global Positioning System

    coastal   allegro
        hydrangea   labyrinth
shrine   entryway
      divine   forearm

the east bay circle: 580 to 24 to 13 to 580

    plasma wind
  deadwood haze
red clay in reverse
  earth unearthed
  voluminous rust
    anguish sky
  sundown coast

circle east 580 to 238 to 880 to 980 to 580 endless

shifting from fourth gear
the clutch is a deep mine
bats vapor from the accelerator
into a dusk
the same wildfire
from which I was woven

Directions, *reprise*

Have the clerk at the Safeway trim the stems of the flowers. She will say the vases are shorter than you remember and cut off more.

    Leave late enough to miss rush hour traffic, but early enough to beat it coming back. Pack warm jackets though it's sunny in Oakland.

On the other side of the San Mateo Bridge, remind everyone the road is winding, to take their eyes off books and devices. Point out the marine layer you knew would still be hanging there mid-morning.

    After taking the right turn find your way through the grounds from memory. Make a u-turn and park where the XII is painted white on the green square curb level.

Feel the wind's blast cracking the door. Scan the hillside for deer. Try and catch a glimpse of ocean through the gray.

    Brush leaves and debris from the markers. Dump the water from Mom's vase in the grass. Watch your wife add fresh flowers to the fake ones, your daughter refill from a bottle.

Realize that Dad's placard doesn't have a vase. Thank your son as he pulls some of the fresh flowers and lays them across the newly engraved bronze.

    Step back and discern the outline and patches in the grass rectangle that was installed almost a year ago. After so many years of visiting one grave with one headstone, squint as you adjust to the presence of the second by its side.

Say a small prayer to yourself. Carry the extra bunch of flowers back to the car, you will bring to Lola & Lolo's wall inside the mausoleum.

    Head to the coast for lunch at Barbara's, seafood with red sauce linguini and clam chowder, hold the bread bowl.

Look out to the horizon from the tables where you would always come after the visits, back then with Mom and Dad and Lola, then for a while with Lola or Dad, and now with only your own family.

foundation

on steel stilts

waiting

for the cement clouds

above

to fall and harden into a

heavy

bed on which the

hundred

year old frame can

rest

St. Mary's Park [Repeat and fade.]

        fourth generation great-grandchildren of this house

dishes break bedrock solid when earth quakes this house

           always red front stairs, tongue of this house

    Lola marks a century in this house

year of birth family planted in this house

           outer mission warm as ilocos norte at this house

    skateboard five minutes to bart from this house

mah jong tiles click clack in this house

           Lolo's ghost patrols oak floors of this house

    slide socks kitchen to bay window in this house

jump back stairs down to the garage of this house

           mom lay cold on the living room floor in this house

    unwrapped presents birthday cakes in this house

alemany flea market uphill to this house

           who will live here when Lola's gone from this house?

    only one place called home, this house

this city this family this blood, this house

So many different addresses growing up.

This is really the only one I remember.

—Denise Maduli-Williams

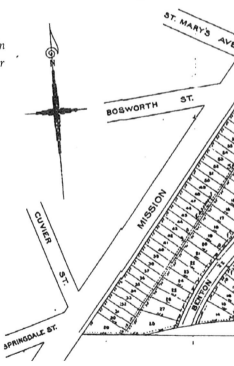

The area upon which our homes are located has had a very colorful history. We call St. Mary's Park, located in the outer Mission District, the Belle of San Francisco for two good reasons: the streets were laid out in the shape of a bell and because we believe it is the most unique neighborhood in the City.

from "A Bell-Shaped Peal from the Past"

Stan Getz & João Gilberto, Getz/Gilberto, Verve Records, 1964.

Map and excerpt courtesy of St. Mary's Park Improvement Club

Brother Noland and the Pacific Bad Boys, *Native News*, The Mountain Apple Company, 1986.

Copyright © 2024 by David Maduli

Alemany Bay Window / Redwood Coast Record Crate
Published by Sampaguita Press
Sampaguita Press LLC
P.O. Box 731305
San Jose, CA 95173

www.SampaguitaPress.com

All rights reserved.

For information about permission to reproduce selections from this book, please contact SampaguitaPress@gmail.com.

Book design by Sampaguita Press
Cover artwork by Jidan Terry-Koon
Author photo by Lara Kaur
Typeset in Cormorant and Brother 1816

ISBN 978-1-965439-00-5 (paperback)
ISBN 978-1-965439-01-2 (ebook)

Land Acknowledgement

This book was written on Ohlone and Bay Miwok lands and produced on Ohlone and Tongva lands.

The staff at Sampaguita Press acknowledge we are settlers on the stolen sacred lands of these Peoples. We remember their connection to these regions and give thanks for the opportunity to live, teach, and learn in their traditional homelands. May we create connections with them, and may we learn Indigenous protocols to become honorable stewards of the land.

We encourage you, Reader, to:

- Amplify the voices of Indigenous people leading grassroots change movements
- Donate your time and money to Indigenous-led organizations
- Politically support the Land Back Movement

In line with these encouragements, Sampaguita Press supports Indigenous art and donates a portion of Press funds raised to Indigenous-led organizations.

In reflecting on our own lives and remembering our family histories, we must remember the legacies of colonialism that we have benefitted from and continue to benefit from as settler-colonialists.

From Palestine to the Philippines, none of us are free until all of us are free.

Stevie Wonder, *Innervisions*, Motown Records, 1976.

"Sometimes the most profound assertions in poetry are the ones made of the smallest gestures. We exist in a world where poetry is often written with a capital P and yet David Maduli crafts a poetry devoid of such trappings and reliant on the quietude of the everyday life. The love of family and place and a grandmother's memory and yes how can we not hold dear the wisdom of a record collection. So put on a record. Open up this book. Know that you are reading the very breath that is life." —**TRUONG TRAN**, author of *book of the other: small in comparison*

"Getting to peer into David Maduli's *Alemany Bay Window* was a gift of poetic oral histories. Maduli's 'house leaks stories' about homes, homelands, streets, and parks and the labyrinth of freeways that connect them. Each poem, a magnet on his Lola's freezer, I found myself traveling in all directions to all the places and emotions that he and his ancestors were willing to take us. By the end of the collection, I was grateful and full of empathetic grief that I longed to hang out in that 'garage [that] has sheltered every member of [t]his family...' / Digging through Maduli's *Redwood Coast Record Crate* of poems, enjoying each designed piece like album covers and liner notes, part of me found myself bobbing my head as I recited each page aloud, smiling at the clever way he sampled his world. The other part of me was in tears seeing the names of Black ancestors violently taken from us. From coming of age to sometimes hope[less] intersections and roads, then fast forward to reflections of gratitude for his family, I found myself journeying the 'bottom of the well' and looking back again and again. Maduli has a beautiful yet painful reflexive way of pursuing 'poetic justice' by weaving his memory with ours and those of the times." —**ALLYSON TINTIANGCO-CUBALES**, Professor of Ethnic Studies, San Francisco State University

"*Alemany Bay Window* is a beautiful series of meditations about family, history, and memory as Maduli's poems trace the journey of his grandparents from the war-torn Philippines to a modest house in the suburbs of San Francisco. As much as it's a love letter to his lola and lolo, the collection is also a series of sensory traces from childhood, grounded in such a vivid specificity of place, you can practically hear the sounds from nearby St. Mary's Playground. For *Redwood Coast Record Crate*, David Maduli spins forth his own liner notes for 16 key albums from his personal audiobiography. Each poem is a wild-style mix of prose and layout that capture the kinetic pulse of hip-hop classics just as well as the modal vibe of a deep-groove jazz pressing. Maduli's *Record Crate* is a delightful ode to a unique, Bay Area heritage of corner tape hustlers, lost underground clubs, and raucous block parties." —**OLIVER WANG**, author of *Legions of Boom: Filipino American Mobile DJ Crews in the San Francisco Bay Area*

"David Maduli's *Alemany Bay Window / Redwood Coast Record Crate* is a dance of what makes our culture: family, place, and music. These poems are meticulously constructed to frame, to contain, a whole world; but they also breathe and expand, crossing in their layers of meaning. The homage, the sample, the quote—everything winks to another hidden ode, showing us the window to homeland and the personal, with the memory of Maduli's Lola and the city that she, and he, love so dearly. These moments bind to us, even as the presence of our loved ones changes. This book: the handhold, the hug, the warm meal at the end of a school day; it peers and pours into each other to make for a polished, heartfelt collection of pure love." —**KEANA AGUILA LABRA**, author of *The Language of Unbreaking*

"Here is a thoroughly rigorous Filipino American hip hop poetics in full effect, in full affect, a heavily gorgeous feat of language that happens only inside the bass-booming quiet of witness. Through these joined joints, from interior mournings of East Oakland through Outer Mission through Ilocos Norte, crossing the Bay Bridge, David Maduli gathers sonic and semiotic through an intimate and expansive atlas of spraycan sighs and saxophone cry-outs, homelands and diasporas, Town and City, lolas and mothers, fathers and lolos, histories and futures, loss and remembrance. On one side, demonstrating the depths of an Alemany elegy on Bataan standard time, and on the other side, inventing and breaking new visual-poetic form to honor universes that groove in and grow out of vinyl records, this double-chapbook / double-album / double-drop / dalawang bagsak talaga, tied tightly together by patient hand and imagination, shall stay hella fresh on bookshelves for generations and generations." —**JASON MAGABO PEREZ**, San Diego Poet Laureate 2023-24

"To read this double-sided wonderwork from David Maduli is to encounter legacy—family and music, visceral histories of emotion and place—via the hands of a poet whose attunement is beyond extraordinary. Through *Alemany Bay Window*, memories call from inside the body of a house, and the stories in their journeying both grieve and refuse loss. In *Redwood Coast Record Crate*, texture is everything as the smallest sonic and visual details become portals of resonance. Together, a singular achievement crossfading the pasts, presents and futures of a tectonic now: when a true DJ scratches the surface, the layers beneath reveal. Studied and innovative, drum-track heavy and tender as the oldest melody, Maduli's work has my head-nod, my turn to *inner vision*, my full applause." —**HARI ALLURI**, author of *The Flayed City*

"David Maduli swings open the back door of his idling Hyundai Excel so we can pop inside to listen to this 'pen's lineage,' the 'ancestories' of elders—Lola and Lolo—reverberating from Bataan to the inside of 'this house' on Alemany as the fog rolls into the city. Then Maduli mashes the gas, hops out to a culdesac party in East Oakland where he deftly spins an 'ode amplified' to hip-hop, soul, jazz and the artistry, collaboration, and community that makes it all happen. Record cover sonnets! Brilliant as the 'inside of two eyes looking into the sun'! I'm a forever fan."—**RACHELLE CRUZ**, author of *God's Will for Monsters*

"*Alemany Bay Window* is tangled histories and foggy memories of a city, a youth, a family, a home. Feels like one long dream; feels like life. *Redwood Coast Record Crate* bursts out loud like when the needle hits the groove. Up close, the topography might seem foreign, but pull back and the parts freely assemble to make their full statement." —**ROGER BONG**, owner of Aloha Got Soul record label and record store in Honolulu

"This isn't just a book: it's an art object. You will read, you will rotate, you will sift through… Stylistic shifts and forms mirror the thematic exploration of memory and identity and music across the A side and B side, where fragments of experience become a more complex whole. The language is measured and deliberate, giving each poem two layers: a written layer and an embedded aural layer that's part of the soundscape. It's the deep groove like the hisses and cracks of a vinyl slipped from a dusted case onto a turntable…it's the perfect kinda analog." —**KEVIN DUBLIN**, author of *Eulogy* and founder of The Living Room SF

Liner Notes

The opening epigraph of *Alemany Bay Window* is Lola Carning's voice from an interview I conducted in 2014, and the closing quote is by my sister Denise from a family oral history collection I compiled around the same time. The first photo of the house is from a family album - photographer unknown, circa 1975. I took the last photo with my phone on the day of Lola's transition, April 2021.

Ancestory: Written after Kevin Dublin and Giovanna Lomanto, with Suheir Hammad's poem "zeitoun" from *The Gaza Suite* (2010) also on my mind. The Q&A in the last five lines takes its influence from the "Voice of the Oracle" game as practiced by Aimé Césaire, Suzanne Césaire and other Black surrealists.

Directions, *continued:* **/ The Park Bell:** The parallel horizontal form echoes the visual movement of wave forms on multitrack mixing software such as Pro Tools. *The Park Bell* refers to the bell at the entrance to the neighborhood and is also the name of the St. Mary's Park Improvement Club's monthly newsletter.

Ode to the Ollie, Landing on a Line by Teju Cole: Dedicated to Jeremy, David, Adam, Mark, Ed, Luis and Corey. Skateboarding every day as a youth was the foundation for so much of how I learned to be in the world. The final line comes from Teju Cole's novel *Open City* (2011).

Oasis Dubplate: Lines in italics are lyrics from Sizzla's "Just One of Those Days" from Robert "Bobby Digital" Dixon's 2004 version of the Queen Majesty riddim.

Jazz Trio on the Uptown Metro: In memory of the godfather Gil Scott-Heron (1949-2011), after "Rivers of My Fathers" from *Winter in America* (1974).

IMPERVIOUS POEM: This piece borrows form and language from then Atlanta Mayor Keisha Lance Bottoms' March 2020 executive order in response to the COVID-19 pandemic. Shout out to the now-defunct *Entropy Magazine* who listed this in their "Best of 2020-21: Favorite Poems Published Online."

Morning; Evening: Written after el maestro Willie Perdomo's poem "Crazy Bunch Barbeque at Jefferson Park" from *Smoking Lovely* (2003).

Ode, Amplified: Written at the Napa Valley Writers' Conference and inspired by Choolwe Kalulu, director of media services at Napa Valley College, who set up and engineered the sound system for the readings that happened each night.

F4ULT/L1NE - REC0RD5.

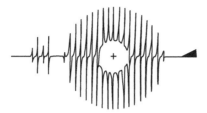

Redwood Coast Record Crate includes a form I've dubbed "record cover sonnets" or "fault/line records." Several years ago as a longtime DJ I began writing poems in the shape of a record jacket, a square in the center of the page. In homage to the source material, I would surround the squares with lyrics, liner notes details, interviews, and additional text referenced or echoed in the music that I would digress into researching. They were initially ekphrastic, responding to the images and textures of the covers and inserts—12" sleeves are so tangible and vibrant. As I continued working with the form, I would find new ways to "break" it. For example, "[Adu]" is reversed with an original poem above and below a center block composed as a cento of lines from Sade. Respect due to the brave work of Theresa Hak Kyung Cha, Layli Long Soldier, Douglas Kearney, Duriel Harris and Kaia Sand who, among others, opened up my feel for the possibilities of the page.

Additional Liner Notes:
[Visage]: Border text is a quote from Dr. Carter G. Woodson's *The Mis-Education of the Negro* (1933).
[pt. reyes]: Lower caption is from *The Cambridge Encyclopedia of Astronomy* (1977).
B L [ ] C K: The last question references the title of Derrick Bell's *Faces at the Bottom of the Well: The Permanence of Racism* (1992).
[Cali]For[Nia]: Nia description comes from *Nguzo Saba* by Maulana Karenga, creator of Kwanzaa in 1966.
[ondes Martenot]: Upper and lower text comes from an essay "The ondes Martenot" by Thomas Bloch, from the CD insert and liner notes of his *Music for Ondes Martenot* (2004), English translation by Susannah Howe.
[Suspended]: Screenplay dialogue comes from the film *The Battle of Algiers* (1966), written by Franco Solinas and directed and co-written by Gillo Pontecorvo, translated from Arabic. The flying names reference the film, Victor LaValle's novel *The Ecstatic* (2003), as well as samples and musicians from the album.

Maxwell, *Urban Hang Suite*, Columbia Records, 1996.

Acknowledgements

This sign post on the journey has been a long time coming—gratitude for the journey. To Maritez, thank you for your heart and mind, mothering, creating, and sharing of dreams. Golden Soundscapes 'til infinity, I love you. To Zuleikha and Apollo, keep being you and sharing your light, you are the best of us. Use these as maps to ground you and blast off to uncharted galaxies.

To Denise, you were the first poet in the fam and always showed me something to strive for growing up and growing into adulthood and parenthood. Thanks for always reading and supporting. To Stephen, Miles & Quincy, I'm proud and honored to call you family. To Lola, your vision was vast enough to encompass dozens of relatives and future generations, thank you for showing me the way to be. Mom and Dad, I miss you both and wish you could celebrate with us. To the Madulis, Sorianos, Fernandezs, Nelsons, Pascuas, Pascuals, and Jusons—ohana.

Gratitude to my brother Hari Alluri. You've been alongside me on this poet path for years and seen me fall off many times, yet never hesitated to rock a session, trade drafts and parse OutKast and Mobb Deep lyrics. This would not be possible without you, pare.

Thank you to my mentors and teachers who imparted gifts of confidence, tools, play and love to get me closer to my voice and art. To Suheir Hammad, your words and lessons are ever-present. To Truong Tran, your courage and curiosity have kept me both grounded and open. To Willie Perdomo, Juan Felipe Herrera, Adrian Matejka, Camille T. Dungy and Ruth Forman, thank you for taking the time to share your process and ask critical questions at the exact times I needed to hear them. You all have been my best teachers in life.

Massive shout to Jidan Terry-Koon, you put your foot in the cover painting! It was critical that the art be envisioned and visualized by family who knew/knows the places, people and eras the work touches on. You were there, and now many years later, here we are.

To the collectives and spaces I'm fortunate to have been part of: The Digital Sala, The Living Room, Sweat Lodge, Cinder Block, Adobe Dojo, VONA/Voices, PROPA and the Knowmadic DJs. Steel sharpens steel, you got a crew you better tell 'em.

Thank you to the Mills College faculty who provided a haven, challenged me and cultivated my work: Elmaz Abinader, Juliana Spahr, Micheline Aharorian Marcom, Ajuan Mance, Achy Obejas and Truong Tran. Thank you to my fellow MFAs, especially multimedia artist and poet Ariel Hanson Strong who hand-printed broadsides of the record cover sonnets and gave them an early feature.

To Shing02, Kirby Dominant, and David Thompson, your decades-long example of prolific art and creative spirit gave me permission to keep going all these years. Dickson Lam and Ken Ja, thank you for everything always. Shout out to friends and fellow artists Karim Scarlata, Isabel Garcia-Gonzales, Aimee Suzara, Kevin Dublin, Chris Starks and Tommy Wong, y'all are fire and I'm honored to be in your company. To the homies Romeo Ponsaran, George Alonzo, Mwapagha Mkonu, Tim Bremner, Wayne Ho, Pankaj Bengani and Gene Kim Whitney, thanks for all your wisdom and encouragement. Big up to Nicholas Basta for your camaraderie and clutch feedback. To Anjoli Roy and Jocelyn Kapumealani Ng, you were "early adopters" of this work, mahalo for providing a platform for poets to shine.

To Sampaguita Press, Keana Aguila Labra and Kelly Ritter, thank you for creating a space for us and giving this work to the community. Maria Bolaños and David Anderson, deep appreciation for your tireless labor, skill and care.

Last but not least, thank you to Truong Tran, Rachelle Cruz, Allyson Tintiangco-Cubales, Jason Magabo Perez, Kevin Dublin, Oliver Wang, Roger Bong and Hari Alluri for your time and generous words.

I grew up reading the liner notes in tapes and records, what a trip to be writing these now. Much love for picking up this book. Bless up.

Many thanks to the editors and staffs of the journals and anthologies in which these poems appeared, often with different titles and in different versions:

COVER: "[Still Traffic]"

Cream City Review: "SF Urban Legend" and the passage "This house," from "The Park Bell" were published as part of a different sequence entitled "microclimates"

Kweli Journal: "[Suspended]" and "IMPERVIOUS POEM No. CV19-19-INF"

Mojave River Review: "thru triple stage darkness"

Sonora Review: "[Asul]"

Spacecraft Project: "Ode, Amplified"

Sparkle & Blink 101: "[pt. reyes]"

Tayo Literary Magazine: "St. Mary's Park *[Tempo rubato.]*"

The /tɛmz/ Review: "Morning; Evening," "[inner vision]"

Tilted House: "B L [ ] C K," "[dropleaf]," "[baseboard]"

Violet Indigo Blue, Etc: "[Dissonance]," "[ondes Martenot]," "[Visage]," for special folio TRANSFIGURATIONS

"Jazz Trio on the Uptown Metro" appears in *Dismantle, An Anthology of Writing from the VONA Writer's Workshop* (Thread Makes Blanket Press, 2014)

"Oasis Dubplate" appears in *The Town: An Anthology of Oakland Poets* (Nomadic Press, 2023)

"St. Mary's Park *[Repeat and fade]*" appears in *Read America(s): An Anthology* (Locked Horn Press, 2016).

About Sampaguita Press

Sampaguita Press is an independent micropress publishing house based in San Jose, California. We publish works by and for artists of color. We acknowledge the intersections of identity and support the LGBTQIA+ folk/x in communities of color as well.

Sampaguita Press was founded in 2021 by poets and creatives who wanted to create a space and platform for ourselves, our peers, and other fellow voices who are underrepresented in mainstream publishing.

We strive to inspire progressive change. We acknowledge that change is made with solidarity. We honor and nurture the relationships between our fellow communities. We especially seek works that broaden perspectives and foster understanding.

We believe in racial and social equity. We acknowledge that Western literature and publishing are still overwhelmingly white spaces, and we are committed to amplifying underrepresented voices by providing attention and care to artists who may not have access to traditional publishing spaces.

We are an intersectionally feminist & womanist, inclusive press. We prioritize artists of color of all genders. We discourage hegemonic narratives; hierarchical structures; and supremacist, assimilationist, and normative messaging.

We are a safe literary & linguistic space, and we welcome book submissions in non-English languages.

We support Indigenous rights and sovereignty over the land known as the United States. Our support goes out to the Indigenous groups everywhere in the world who have been harmed, silenced, and displaced. We encourage our readers to learn about and support Indigenous Peoples.

Buju Banton, *'Til Shiloh*, Island Records, 1995.

About the Artist

Artist, organizer, and community builder Jidan Terry-Koon hails from four generations of Chinese families, from Toi Shan and Yueng Zhou respectively, living and working in the San Francisco Bay Area. This history helps shape her passion for racial and economic justice in the context of harmony with the natural world.

Grounded in grassroots community organizing, she has played critical roles in the creation of several organizations focused on these causes, including the Climate Justice Alliance and Power California. She seeks to practice kindness and inter-generational connections as central tools for change.

Based in Oakland, Jidan enjoys hiking, swimming, any kind of art, and family time.

Joni Mitchell, *Blue*, Reprise Records, 1971.

About the Author

David Maduli's work, often inflected by many years as a public school teacher and DJ, has received the Joy Harjo Poetry Prize. Born in San Francisco, he is a father of two and a longtime resident of East Oakland where he completed his MFA at Mills College with a fellowship in Community Poetics.

His work has been showcased at events such as SF Litquake and RAWdance's *Step/Song/Story* series, and his poems appear widely in journals and anthologies including *Sonora Review*, *Cream City Review*, and *Kweli Journal*. He has received residencies and fellowships at VONA/Voices, Las Dos Brujas, Martha's Vineyard Institute of Creative Writing and Napa Valley Writers' Conference.

In addition to his work as an educational leader and researcher, he is an instructor of poetry craft and literature in the MFA in Writing program at Lindenwood University.

Lauryn Hill, *The Miseducation of Lauryn Hill*, Ruffhouse Records, 1998.

RESPECT TO THE DJs: Zita, Mpenzi, Son of Jules, VNA, Icewater, Crimson, Platurn, Apollo, ShortKut, Sake One, Willie Maze, Tim Diesel, Namane, Eleven, Henroc, Fuze, Pam the Funkstress aka Purple Pam (RIP), Lovelee, Neta, Ross Hogg, Mr. E, Mind Motion, Joe Quixx, King Tech, Touré, TD Camp, Wisdom, D-Sharp, Dedan, Daniela, B-Love, Doc Fu, Stef (RIP), G-Smoove, Digumsmak, Top Bill, Dai-Nasty, Spin Master A-1, Red-i, Soul Flower, Coop D'Ville, Jah Yzer, I-Vier, Irie Dole, Lenoir, Toks, Wonway, Hector, Fflood (RIP), Black, Cecil, Cali, heyLove, Nina Sol, soul.profess, Kaution, Oliver Orzal, Treat-U-Nice, ThatGirl, OwlBoogie, Herb Digs, Hen10, Hakobo, Proof, King Most, PantyROBber, D-Real, Rani D, Mel, Bency, Beatnick, Solace, Riddm, Discaya, Donovan, Dion Decibels, Delrokz, Odiaka, Delgado, Serg, Saurus, Hen Boogie, Bizarro, True Justice, 3rd Degree, Profeta, ill Equipt, Solomon (RIP), Spair, Ren the Vinyl Archaeologist, Leydis, Gravy, Green B, J-Boogie, Brigidope, (Uncle) Mike, Macapuno, Mark Maiden, Solo, Eric Rukis, Roza, Ant-1, Expo, KJ Butta, Seeko, Chia, K-ing, Monkey, Toki, Marloca, Ms. Angel, Tittahbyte, Revise, Roger Bong, Oliver Seguin, Basta, Kush Arora, Maneesh the Twister, Zen, Shadow, Davey D, Weyland, O-Dub, Double O, Matthew Africa (RIP), AsceticFish (RIP), Phatrick, un.d.fine, Tap10, Aebl Dee, NeoGeo, BlaQwest, Jenicyde, Beatnok, Mr. Lucky, Journee, Dash Eye, Wundrkut (RIP), Stevelder, Audio1, Drez, Cut Chemist, Nu-Mark, Dusk (RIP), Vinroc, Neil Armstrong, Celskii, Deeandroid, Cutso, Umami, GoldenChyld, Emancipation, Rimarkable, Lady Ryan, Dredd, mOma, Quartermaine, Jaycee, Jamad, Chrissy Murderbot, Paul Nice (RIP), Q-Bert, D-Styles, Mixmaster Mike, Swift Rock (RIP), J.Rocc, Rhettmatic, Babu, Melo-D, Icy Ice, Symphony, Derrick D, Kon & Amir, A-Trak, Frankie Knuckles, Larry Levan, Masters at Work, ?uestlove, Muro, Craze, Z-Trip, Nickodemus, Jazzy Jeff, Spinna, Rich Medina, Stretch Armstrong, Bobbito, Kid Koala, Peanut Butter Wolf, K-Salaam, Rob Swift, Roc Raida, Mista Sinista, Mr. DJ, Mister Cee, Clark Kent, Ron G, Funkmaster Flex, Tony Toca, Kid Capri, Mark the 45 King, Eclipse, Cut Creator, K-Rock, Screw, Daryl, Mannie Fresh, Quik, D-Nice, Maseo, Ali Shaheed Muhammad, Premier, Pete Rock, Jam Master Jay (RIP), Terminator X, Spinderella, Jazzy Joyce, Cash Money, Marley Marl, Kool DJ Red Alert, Grandmaster Flash, Kool Herc. The DJ is archive.

Nas, *Illmatic*, Columbia Records, 1994.

Respect to the power strip, the extension cord—
        those immigrant inventions

I see you zip ties, I see you gaff tape, tucking away cords how families
        conceal secrets, preventing stumbles but still perceptible
        underfoot, fault lines inching for years then erupting unwarned

Gratitude to the sound engineer! Thank you to the thumb and forefinger,
        the twist of knobs EQs and frequencies, also bent
        to turn pages of favorite comics, sign debts, brush tears,
        text loved ones, tease lovers

All these, all you, praise due for the One—through whose hand
        these waves of sound connected and tuned—

Ode, Amplified

Appreciations first and foremost to the loudspeakers, the active
        monitor 6,000-watt boom to fill cave or cavernous sky, the way
        young siblings can empower a morning, expand
        an afternoon, explode a summer bedtime

Much love to the microphones: handheld wireless lavalier cardioid
        dynamic unidirectional, what inanimate object can come
        this close to a kiss?

Shout out to the light-emitting diodes in the dark,
        phosphorescent dance on the mixing board
        how century-old Lola's vital signs looked from the
        St. Luke's bed after her second stroke

Thank God for the reach into the bag, the extra set of rechargeable
        batteries, cylinders of prayer in hand

Can't forget the speaker stands, tripedal alloy with the ability to hold
        unknown heaviness, the way Dad endured after Mom's death—
        hydraulic elevation, steel stability, hidden hollowness

The cables, the cables! XLR RCA Aux, ah the satisfying clack of the 1/4"
        plug in its connection, the way Lolo affixed the clip in his rifle as
        he hid under the table, the first round slid in the chamber while the
        Bataan Death March rivered around his abandoned barrio

No recording I've heard captures his sound as well as this one…Part of the reason is that the recording was made at a tape speed of 30 inches per second, instead of the usual 15.

To understand

and be understood

i only want to provide a hint of the brush's edge. i try and work as if it is décollage, as if each stroke was torn from a magazine or a piece of someone's heart. imagine that the finished work is a close up—a begonia's stamen, the skin of a freshwater stingray. why these colors specifically? do you ever have a craving for a certain cuisine? those four jet black splotches, they are powerful, no? there are times when extreme contrast is needed, is necessary. then when the whole piece is framed with the enormity of outer space, we have to ask, were those painted on top, or are they eternity reaching through the canvas?

is a kind of peace.

    Um cantinho,

      um violão

    Esse amor,

      uma canção

    Pra fazer feliz

      A quem se ama

WHAT ARE YOU DOING
MODERN MAN
EVERYDAY I WATCH YOU MOVE AT
LIGHTNING SPEED
SIT DOWN, HOLD ON STEADY
BIG SHIP SAILING ON THE OCEAN
BIG SHIP SAILING ON THE OCEAN
BIG SHIP SAILING ON THE OCEAN

WORDS & MUSIC BY FREDDIE McGREGOR
PRODUCED & ARRANGED BY BROTHER NOLAND AND GAYLORD HOLOMALIA
Lead Vocals & Guitars — Brother Nola[nd]
Bass & Vocals — Kata Maduli
Vocals, Whistles, Percussion — Jeff Gerona
Synthesizer Programming and B-3 — Gaylord Holomalia
Horn Arrangements — Brother Nolan[d] and Gaylord Holomalia

Vocals and Rhythm Tracks, Overdubs [at] Lahaina Sound
Additional Overdubs & Mixing at Sea-West Studios/Hawaii

Kata Maduli, the next of the original bad boys, has been involved with Brother Noland in one way or the other for the last few years. His musical career began at the ripe old age of 9 while he was still in elementary school.

Kata's musical journey has taken [her] through many different instrum[ents as] well as bands. He has been fortu[nate to] have the opportunity to perform [with the] likes of Stevie Wonder, Ricky Nelson & the Stone Canyon Band, Rufus, Tower of Power, Sammy Davis and David Williams to name a few. His experience with local groups has been extensive in that he has played with the likes of Loyal Garner, Cecilio & Kapono, Nohelani Cypriano, Kalapana and Iva Kinimaka. These experiences have taken Kata into different musical fields as well as new performing experiences. Everything from major arena events to a small cocktail lounge, has been put into his musical bag and these

brother noland bounds from the drum skin like a trampoline, red anthurium loafers to match his guitar, hibiscus cape wings open floating honolulu's electric blue. open the news inside, there is uncle kata squinting with big glasses, raglan sleeves pushed up to his elbows posing in front of the vw van with curtains. later the pacific bad boys flood the club with freddie's big question. the theory of relativity is a bay area bass rerouting wavelengths all along kalakaua avenue. modern man you nah ready for this lava breeze. your ship is nuclear submarine our ship is solar oceania

I have the following Brother Nolan[d] albums:
☐ Speaking Brown
☐ Paint the Island
☐ Pacific Bad Boy
☐ Native News
☐ None of the above

My favorite song by Brother Nolan[d]
☐ Pua Lane
☐ Coconut Girl
☐ Look What They've Done
☐ Choose your own: _____

I buy my records & cassettes at (store name): _____

To all Kata's students who help keep up his chops
To all the people who support us on the West Coast
To all the people who support us in the Islands
To Anybody we missed — Many Thanks
KAPIOLANI MEDINA — Heaven and earth last forever because they are unborn, so ever living and of course
POMAIKA'IMAHINA — Jewel of light shine through my heart

Ali La Pointe ▶

Homunculus ▶

    OMAR
Men have two faces, the one that laughs
and the one that cries

Anthony James ▶

Colonel Mathieu ▶

Georgia Ann Muldrow ▶

Otis Jackson, Jr. ▶

seagull of a boy in flight, baseball cap points yesterday rubber soled toe taps tomorrow, steel girders outside, concrete columns inside, jalousie windows vent the emptiness out, pavement below catching shadows, grey tshirt the only chain mail armor between skin and life, limbs grow past the length of jeans, years reach in all directions, motion is the same as stillness,

Uncle Arms ▶

Ishkabibble ▶

Ledric Mayo ▶

Petit Omar ▶

Maximilian ▶

forever is an instant, four feet of sky is still freedom

    ALI
They sent you?

Fela Anikulapo-Kuti ▶

Nabisase ▶

    OMAR
Yeah, so? Here.

Malik El-Shabazz ▶

Slick Rick The Ruler ▶

Dante Bezé ▶

Fender Rhodes, Moog Bass,

T.O.N.T.O. synthesizer, Hammond organ,

Hohner clavinet, drums,

shaker, harmonica,

handclaps

if this was a superhero storyboard the beam bending skyward would be lasers to slice concrete or freeze rays or a memory-washer but nah, this is real life. corals twist from the desert floor, pyramids oxidize in the fog between fort point and fort mason, slate is the color of everything, most days the timbre too. inside the gate the three patrol—silence, despair, apathy—arms the same oblique angle that the laser pierces the beige, but i already told you it's not that. the beam, despite streaks of rust and patina, is the only true thing that matters: it is the inside of two eyes looking into the sun

(Repeat several times)

(Repeat to end)

REPEAT and FADE

FADE

REPEAT – MUSIC – FADE

REPEAT and FADE

FADE

bro, that's your beautiful family right there
you know that?
that's you
and i knew you before all that
before her
i knew you after some shit went down
and you didn't know what was gonna happen next
you didn't even know what you
were doing and where you were going
and now here you are
so don't fuck this up
because if you fuck this up
it fucks me up

the opening synths of "i got five on it"
echo up to the hills
this better be the remix with richie rich!
someone shouts
and of course it is

Morning; Evening

—after Willie Perdomo

the east oakland culdesac party
for hector's 40th: ah man that blocked off
dead end street might actually be
a barrio in ilocos or guadalajara or east los
or east oakland where it really is
when the dj throws on bell biv devoe even
abuelita is gettin down on the walkway
up the porch and there's a taco truck parked
and pancit palabok and pulled pork with king's
hawaiian bread and mac n cheese

the opposite of the scene at mosswood park
that morning when you took your kids to play and a group of way-too-comfortables were spread out
on a blanket with a box of peet's coffee and another box of la farine pastries hella taking their shoes
off and lounging on the spongy playground surface
encroaching on the swingset zone so much you're practically tripping over
them as you try and push your son and you wish the angle would be just right
on the upswing his foot would catch a laughing
newcomer on his upturned chin

o, but hector's party, big al bellows you into a bear hug
pours you a paloma
points you to the table where your wife is wiping
your daughter's face and your son is balancing his way
on the cinder blocks circling the tree and chuckles:

wrote the vows the night before to read on the beach
at sunset can't remember the exact phrasing my laptop got stolen years later can't even recall
a single word but i remember the surf was up that day a few locals were out in the bowl
damn the water must have felt like floating on a quasar the sand
under my feet was rough enough to keep me present there was this one palm tree
that was really leaning growing sideways up and over the shorebreak its shadow just went forever
the kahu said something about mom how she was there with us
the last time i talked to her she had just bought the dress she was going to wear
for it and he also talked about the expanse of the ocean how from this coast the next

every winter was a war she said, i want to get what's mine. every day is christmas, and every night is new year's eve. he tastes her kiss, her kisses are not wine. it's like the weather one day chicken next day feathers.   i'm never going to see you again i wish you could meet my new friends. azul es el color del rojo cielo, matador no puedo seconder mi temor. i've got a bullet to spare, don't wanna send it your way. you cut into my life. wider than victoria lake, taller than the empire state. do you really want to know she said. natural as the way we came to be. grandma came to see something she could not believe

: a statement telling someone that you will definitely do something or that something will definitely happen in the future

: a reason to expect that something will happen in the future

: an indication of something favorable to come

land was three thousand miles away and how that could be
a metaphor for something and your feet were bare too and I could see
greenish gold flecks in your eyes and smell the gardenias in your hair
the kahu's daughter came forward to offer the leis and the homie
taking photos was waist deep in the waves trying to get the best angle
and when i think about that day i am grateful for him because he cared enough
to go for it without tripping off sand and saltwater in his shoes or the seaspray all over his lenses
or the change of clothes he didn't bring
and years later i hope we can put as much into this as he did

cloudarch   sailfire   goldengate   zigzagzig

slumberfall   humankine   butterflytrap

stolenova   tearlock   sunfetti   pearlscape

overcast   gardenyears   heartwolves

dropleaf   fleshache   cinderblock   clockwork

candlestick   songyears   sidewinders
e y e w i n g s c h a l k b o d y s t a r h o m e
l a n d h o m e l a n d

homelandhomelandhomelandhomelandh

To understand how the ondes Martenot works, we need to look at an acoustic phenomenon. The string of an instrument playing the note A has a frequency of 440 Hz, i.e. it vibrates back and forth 440 times per second. Depending on the speed of this vibration, the note (frequency) is low or high. The radio used by Maurice Martenot only worked at a very high frequency, emitting an ultrasonic note inaudible to the human ear (80000 Hz).

THEATRE DES TODES

if ~~broken~~ was a landscape this would be the coordinates. how else to paint ~~mountains~~ so jagged but to use ~~knives~~ for brushes? on this planet they spire so menacingly ~~they~~ peak in flames. ~~sky~~ and coal are the same, the only ~~light~~ glares from glacier, its hunger ~~powers~~ the abbatoir just beyond the rise. treelines materialize to defy the ~~fire~~ and ~~ice~~, multiply the serration. sheets of ~~broken~~ glass extend their palms to guide ~~you~~ into oblivion. upon entry ~~your~~ ~~perception~~ becomes pixelated. there is ~~comfort~~ in freeze, ~~caress~~ in stab. ~~beauty~~ in deformity, ~~love~~ in destruction, ~~love~~ in end, ~~love~~ in love

treelines materialize to defy the ~~fire~~ and ~~ice~~, multiply the serration. on this planet they spire so menacingly ~~they~~ peak in flames. upon entry ~~your~~ ~~perception~~ becomes pixelated. ~~sky~~ and coal are the same, the only ~~light~~ glares from glacier, its hunger ~~powers~~ the abbatoir just beyond the rise. there is ~~comfort~~ in freeze, ~~caress~~ in stab. if ~~broken~~ was a landscape this would be the coordinates. sheets of ~~broken~~ glass extend their palms to guide ~~you~~ into oblivion. ~~beauty~~ in deformity, ~~love~~ in destruction, ~~love~~ in end, ~~love~~ in love. how else to paint ~~mountains~~ so jagged but to use ~~knives~~ for brushes?

Fin-
de-
Siècle

To obtain an audible sound, he used heterodyning (which musicians use when tuning to another instrument) - producing a beat frequency by the combination of two oscillations of slightly different frequency in order to generate a third, whose value is the mathematical difference between the first two. The note A, for example, can be produced by the simultaneous inaudible frequencies of 80000 and 80440 Hz. The first frequency is fixed and never changes, while the second is variable, modified by the performer who plays the instrument either via a *keyboard* or by moving a wire known as a *ribbon*.

PT. 01   PT. 02

this is the floor. no matter if it was the second or third, it always felt like ground. you'd abandon your heels and we would trace barefoot secrecies, time cross-hatched us into endless rows of inter-locking diamonds the rug knew by heart

this is the wall. it rose from the gift of the ground to a place beyond our vision, clouded even when close up. it is the thing we invested the most into, and constantly fed it divided and multiplied, a mitosis of memory until it was the only thing that we could recognize. it fills our throats, every closet & crawlspace, this ornate iron lung

PT. 03   PT. 04

DISPLACEMENT AND ENTITLEMENT A PANDEMIC; DECLARING HIS NURSE COUSIN'S BANDANA AN INSUFFICIENT BARRIER FOR INFECTIOUS DROPLETS AND ANTI-ASIAN HATE; DECLARING THE PRESENCE OF NATIONAL GUARD TANKS TO DISTRIBUTE AID AN EMERGENCY IN EXISTENCE; DECLARING THE TERM "NEW NORMAL" A WIDESPREAD MISNOMER THAT MUST CEASE, FOR WHAT CRISES SHOULD BE DEEMED "NORMAL" HERETOFORE OR TODAY? WITHIN WHICH TERRITORIAL JURISDICTIONS OF LANGUAGE IS "NORMAL" NOT SYNONYMOUS WITH OPPRESSION? IN ACCORDANCE WITH THE AUTHORITY VESTED IN THE UPRISING SEAS, IT IS HEREBY ORDERED CHILDREN BE HUGGED TIGHT, TAUGHT CHESS AND READ BOOKS BY OCTAVIA BUTLER, THAT QUARANTINE MATES DISTANT AND NEAR DANCE REGGAETON, DRINK AND MAKE LOVE, THAT FLAMES BE FOR COOKING AND FEEDING FAMILY UNTIL THEY BECOME FLAMES FOR CAPITOL BUILDINGS, THAT THE CITY ERUPT WITH MARIPOSA LILIES AND SEA OTTERS, THAT THE STOCK MARKET CLOSE FOREVER; PURSUANT TO UNIVERSAL LAW, THE ANCESTORS, AND THE APOCALYPTIC SNARE REVERB OF DILLA'S "FALL IN LOVE," THIS POEM IS EFFECTIVE IMMEDIATELY AND SHALL STAY IN EFFECT UNTIL FURTHER NOTICE.

City of Quarantine
State of Emergency

Department of Poetic Justice

IMPERVIOUS POEM No. CV19-93-INF

DECLARING GROCERY RUNS NOW A PERIL FOR ALL, ALBEIT NOT SO PERILOUS AS FOR ANY BLACK YOUTH WITH A HOODIE; AS SUCH, WHILE IDLING IN THE TRADER JOE'S PARKING LOT STREAMING A BROADCAST FROM JAMAICA THE SWELL OF BACKGROUND VOCALS ON THE CHORUS OF "DESTINY" WOULD BRING THE DRIVER TO TEARS, THE SAX PLAYER'S STOICISM WOULD LEND THE NECESSARY COURAGE TO STAND IN A LINE TWENTY DEEP, THE SMALL YET INADEQUATE BLESSING OF ANTIBACTERIAL WIPES DISTRIBUTED AT THE DOOR LIKE RAFFLE TICKETS; WHEREAS ONLY A FEW INCHES DISTANCING HIM AND THE SHOPPER WHO INSISTED ON REACHING IN FRONT FOR THE MARINARA JAR REMINDS HIM OF THE REDWOOD TRAIL THE DAY BEFORE, WHEN THE JOGGER BARRELED BETWEEN HIS SMALL CHILDREN, THE SWEAT THAT TINGED THE MOUNTAIN AIR, THE UNUSUAL CONDITION OF

Jazz Trio on the Uptown Metro

solo ends   spotlight empties
the light remains
on the edges of a solar system
drummer bass player and keyboardist
drive a city bus full of survivors
through the rain
let rain come now let it
waterfall

no traffic lights now
no traffic we ride now

no city   no street
three musicians and wind

no bus now they steer us forward
steel water our eyes concrete air our throats
a river of wounds rushing down

no band now
drum becomes a hand smoothing hair
bass crumbles into gravel
keys snow flurries

no bodies now
no clouds   no sky
we are whispers

—*for Gil Scott-Heron*

If life is prison

the reel-to-reel's radioactivity is your jungle gym, the glowing bounce of the analog meters is your babysitter, the drum machine is your drum, your striped shirt externalizes the young horizons revolving inside, your brother two grades behind but taller and moodier, intent on tying his left tennis shoe, ignores the shoulder-height stack on the floor, the closest shape in the foreground his bare right toes, you play for hours, years, oblivious to the panorama stretching behind you, overlooking green-gold foothills, flatland homes, the estuary beyond, static hiss of a distant island. the haze robing the bay is god's graphic design

then the music

Day 5 *(Purpose)*: To make our collective vocation the building and developing of our community in order to restore our people to their traditional greatness.

is the yard time

BREONNA   TAYLOR   AMADOU   DIALLO
MANUEL   LOGGINS   JR.   RONALD
MADISON   JAMES   BRISSETTE   EMMITT
TILL TRAVARES MCGILL GEORGE FLOYD
TIMOTHY   THOMAS   TIMOTHY   RUSSELL
ELIJAH   MCCLAIN   PHILANDRO   CASTILE
AIYANA   STANLEY   JONES   SEAN   BELL
TAMIR RICE ERVEN JEFFERSON OUSMANE
ZONGO   ORLANDO   BARLOW   AARON
CAMPBELL   KENDREC MCDADE   TIMOTHY
STANSBURY JR. JOHN CRAWFORD III
RAMARLEY   GRAHAM   KIMANI   GREY
MERON   TILLMAN   VICTOR   STEEN   STEVEN
EUGENE WASHINGTON ALONZO ASHLEY
WENDELL   ALLEN   VONDERRIT   MYERS
JR.   OSCAR   GRANT   MICHAEL   BROWN
ALBERTA   SPRUILL   LAQUAN   MCDONALD
CAREY   SMITH-VIRAMONTES   JEFFREY
HOLDEN   TRAYVON   MARTIN   QUSEAN
WHITTEN   ALEX   NIETO   ERIC   GARNER

> balancing on chords i climbed the tip top
> note and could not hold back the abyss
> from circling the times slipping from my
> pores my lungs took their gadgetry and left
> arriving on the wrong train at the wrong
> altitude could not recognize my own voice
> holding me the spooling two-inch tape
> ready to catch me on the left and right my
> sister reaching to me with cymbals for
> hands my wife unzipping a viola from her
> neck my fathers and sons handing me their
> chorus on the hood of a squad car and we
> jammed like the cliff never existed til the
> chasm opened us and we walked inside
> together while the metronome shed its
>   skin
>   swinging
>   its newfound
>   pendulum
>   like a
>   blacksmiths
>   hammer

B
L

What isn't there and always was?

What does pigment begin?

For what must we all pay?

inside clasped hands, pen's lineage, asphalt yawning across time, the inhale of space, holes in i love you, god in her leather executive chair, tinted limo idling downstairs, night waves, eels roiling in and out of the surface, ocean's conscience, gray before white, hooded sweatshirt on a target, the president's shoe shine, the ski mask way, what candles reach for, unraveled cassette tape, junkyard brimming with tires, tangle of hair after restless sleep, topography of vinyl, depression's palette, fishnet interlacing skin, queen of spades, jack of clubs, signature arched glissando, the soil inside

C
K

What's in the bottom of the well looking back?

who feels it,
knows

D. Germain
Steely & Clevie
Mafia & Fluxy
Sly & Robbie
"Coxsone" Dodd
"Bobby Digital" Dixon
"Rude Boy" Kelly

from my peripheral i see you even with eyelashes to cheekbones your hunger precedes you go throw the law at my spine, heart arrested soul ribcaged stolen untold tomorrows give you the kilimanjaro of my shoulder the mangroves of my mane to let you know this road no côte d'ivoire chart passage through mist this river braids years, australopithecus risen to diamonds in the sky, seven dromedaries thru the needle's eye, gather all this atlas in my profile 'til shiloh thunderclouds crown me with grayscale fists—so tell me, sir, what's the pantone number of your greatest fear?

Kette Drum 72

Tempo 87

Swing Easy 84

Arab Attack 87

Champion 90

Far East 68

I could go on and on the *full* has never been told

[Version 3]

Ten years from now, rewind—you are standing in this spot again, this patio remade into a beer garden with picnic benches and that bean bag game, Cuba Libres replaced by a mixologist painstakingly applying drops of bitters, the mix of reggae 45s replaced with a football game on too many flat screens, undulating shades from across the African diaspora replaced with the mayor high heel-stepping through the alley waving to a councilman. This is some time after various complaints from neighbors will shut the spot down multiple times, after Fish will get hit with fire code violation after violation, after city hearings with a swath of nightlife stalwarts and the greater community will show out to support. After Fish will mysteriously fall down some back stairs to his and Oasis' end.

Just

one

of

those

days

The chorus breaks   everyone is singing

Why does it have to be this way?

You sing too   The   same   sea   flailing

Can't tell you to go, can't tell you to stay

in the same tempest

Just one of those days

—Tonight as you peace out Lenoir is running bashment riddims, the mass of bodies a palpitating heart. In the Sentra realize you somehow left your jacket. Slumping back against the headrest, stare at the number on your phone.

Am I too humble or ignorant?   *Things began to fade,*

[Version 2]

Rewind to last weekend when you and Mpenzi ended the night juggling
Beres Hammond tunes, the man with the grey-flecked beard leaning on the patio
bar ambled over to nod, *You made me feel like I was back home*, before fading
to the alley, stars sparking somewhere above the amber street light's radiation

—Toks drops back to the first pounding keys *Even my heart*
   of Sizzla Kalonji's "Dry Cry" *cries*
     Fists and palms clatter
    on the corrugated steel *but who*
       siding, on any wood panel *cares*
         within arm's reach

Whose fault,
      That phantasmic falsetto *no one*
  You close your eyes,

but myself
    everyone is moving

   including you The chorus breaks everyone is singing

Why does it have to be this way?
      You sing too

Can't tell you to go, can't tell you to stay

Oasis Dubplate

—Downtown Oakland, circa 2002

[Version 1]

You good, fam? In a fluid motion the lanky shadow with a Basquiat
crown backlit by garnet lamps tops off two Rum & Cokes, pops open
a Red Stripe for good measure, slides you one of them and the brown bottle,
clinks his glass to yours. Rewind to the night he first hired the Knowmadic

I'm

crew, you remember he chuckled, *David too, but call me Ras David.*
His father is Fessehaye, Fish for short, owner of the landmark Eritrean
restaurant and bar in The Town. You shoulder no record bag tonight but
you're here—to not think about the months it's been since you visited

missing

your parents, or the number saved in your phone that you're hoping you
don't call later, or the state testing you have to proctor the next day. From
the shouts and migration of bodies from the bar, Toks or Fuze must be up
now on the patio. You sidestep the gauntlet between the two lines

youuuu

for bathrooms that will overflow later, through the narrow passage
to the rear where smoke is prevalent, adjacent downtown buildings seem
to tower even higher, and reverberations off them create a flying ricochet.
Sure enough Lenoir is on the mic screaming *PULL UPP—*

June 22, 1971

Dear California —
I'm coming home.

—after Joni

to call it midnight would be cliché. cobalt matches the texture and intensity but the hue is still too bright. cerulean sounds like it, slow and low, but same problem as the previous. indigo is more accurate but duke and nina already did that best. navy gives it military connotations. deep, dark, those are nothing but nickel and dime adjectives. let's just say it's the opposite of azure: the infinity of cloudless sky, the early mornings you walk outside and fill lungs the size of your body, reach fingertips to press the firmament, and on the first step feel like you can run and run and run forever. the opposite of that blue.

[Asul]

19 hours, 19 minutes, right ascension

Mullard Radio Astronomy Observatory, Cambridge, England
Arecibo Radio Observatory, Puerto Rico

why did mom love lighthouses so much? maybe the tangling of safety and danger intermittent promise of beacon above dusk waters lapping night coast, faithfulness and blindness, candle on a sandstone altar, inseam of submerged fault lines, loneliness washing into the sea, loneliness washing back, vantage from which the unknown swells, maybe she imagined ocean as the future, over time it just looked like eternity, endlessness of a sea lion's savannah and she never heard death over moon's pacific insomnia twisting sheets of whitewater on the ash rock bed surrounding the point

fig. 6.7: Successive pulses from the first pulsar discovered, CP 1919, are here superimposed vertically. The pulses occur every 1.337 seconds. They are caused by a rapidly-spinning neutron star.

I was hopeless   *now I'm on Hope Road*

to tell him not to stand here or go yonder. He will find his 'proper place' and will stay in it.

> this classroom, among many rows & rows. this last row, this desk. etched into its layers of particle board & veneer: my face. the contours of it, my hair distended towards the edges. syrah from an upset glass, this is what i am: stain. next year, next kid who sits in this seat will find me here, peer into blotches of time and song. folklore's faded infrastructure, wood grain's rhythm. she will reach for the number two pencil haloed above my head, despite its worn point & no eraser, she will raise it & write to me or to you words of scrape & char & cement & sawdust letter after letter hymns of drip & collapse

When you control a man's thinking you do not have to worry about his actions. You do not have

You do not need to send him to the back door. He will go without being told. In fact, if there is no back door, he will cut one for his special benefit. His education makes it necessary. (1933)

What you throw out   *comes back to you, star*

begin like a violin

all the words

[40 SIDE NORTH 1-5]

from the middle of the intersection it appears that two sidewalks converge to a distant point directly in the center of his eyebrows a lamp post bisects his left pupil or maybe just a reflection of the mustard sun from windshields of parked cars sinking under his eyelids like metal tears the only motion is the late model boxframe elongated to a blur from philtrum through right earlobe then gone a passing throught unworded his slight frown reveals no teeth or teleology only three letters in lowercase old english he is young but does not smile as the street looks through him into you

[41 SIDE SOUTH 6-10]

end like leviathan

past the margins

◀ 10

undulates eyes closed
hears you clearly
as if sharing

the same anemone, nods
yes, this is ocean
moon is just beyond

next tidal wave

       —for Zita

Sly & Robbie at The Justice League

—San Francisco, circa 2000

ever been in proximity
of bass
so wide and endless

you lava into it?
boiling and
shattering

from heavy
speakerboxxxes
planted on stage

black limestone cliffs
dunbar & shakespeare
strike-slip faults colliding

wave you fragile
epipelagic
kelp forest in a storm

oh mami wata them two
rhythm section
for a galaxy

pressure gauge gone
you lean whisper
the siren holding your hand

Contents

- 8   Sly & Robbie at The Justice League
  - 10   [Still Traffic]
  - 11   [Visage]
  - 12   [pt. reyes]
  - 13   [Asul]
- 14   Oasis Dubplate
  - 17   [Grayscale]
  - 18   B L [ ] C K
  - 19   [Dissonance]
  - 20   [Cali]For[Nia]
- 21   Jazz Trio on the Uptown Metro
- 22   IMPERVIOUS POEM No. CV19-93-INF
  - 24   [baseboard]
  - 25   [ondes Martenot]
  - 26   [dropleaf]
  - 27   [Adu]
- 28   Morning; Evening
  - 30   [inner vision]
  - 31   [Suspended]
  - 32   [Big Ship]
  - 33   [Brush, Edge]
- 34   Ode, Amplified

for A&Z
who asked why we have
so many records

Hang on to the world as it spins around

—Donny Hathaway

*update old records / tune around the verses /
fast time and swing out / head set in a groove*

—Harryette Mullen

redwood coast record crate

David Maduli

Sampaguita
Press

Milton Keynes UK
Ingram Content Group UK Ltd.
UKHW051342251024
2383UKWH00056B/244